CANADA'S NATIONAL PARKS

CLB 2213
© 1988 Colour Library Books Ltd, Godalming, Surrey, England
Photographs pages 17, 18 and 19: E. Sieber
Printed and bound in Barcelona, Spain by Cronion, S.A.
All rights reserved
ISBN 0 86283 614 X

Dep. Leg. B-4189-88

CANADA'S NATIONAL PARKS

**Text by
Bill Harris**

*Photography by
William Curwen and Nick Meers*

Bramley Books

NATIONAL PARKS OF CANADA

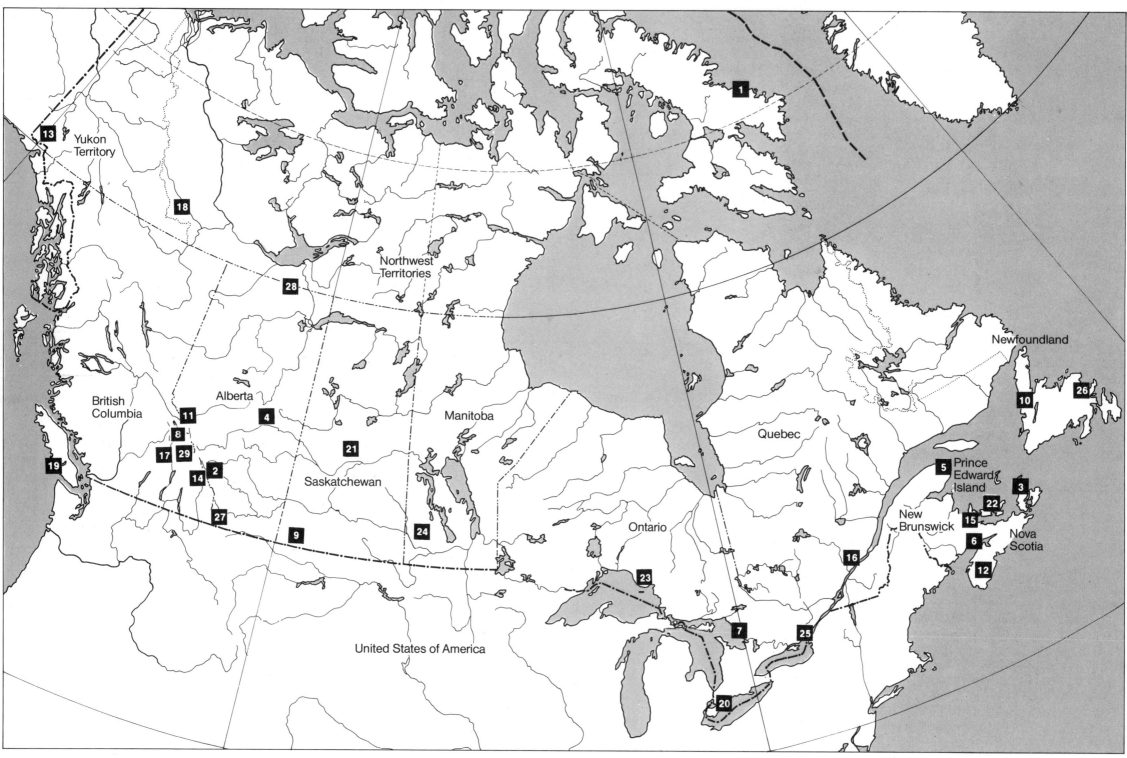

"They rose bold and abrupt five or six thousand feet from the wooded country at their feet, the western verge of the plains the elevation of which was over three thousand feet additional above the sea, and formed a long unbroken line across our path. ... Everything was imposing. And these, too, were ours, an inheritance as precious, if not as plentiful in corn and milk, as the rich plains they guarded. For mountains elevate the mind and give an inspiration of courage and dignity to the hardy races who own them and who breathe their atmosphere."

Anyone seeing the Rocky Mountains for the first time from the edge of the plains in Alberta could easily conjure up the emotion of those words. They could have been written last week. But, in fact, they were written in the last century. They are a record of the first impressions of the expedition of Sandford Fleming which crossed the continent in 1872 to map a route for the Canadian Pacific Railroad.

The route Fleming picked across the Rockies was directly responsible for Canada's first national park. And that, in part, is why the area has hardly changed in the more than one hundred years since the railroad explorers first crossed and recrossed the mountains, rejected the Yellowhead Pass and moved further south to Kicking Horse Pass, which an earlier party of explorers had recommended.

The construction crews that followed them discovered wonderful hot springs in one of the most beautiful spots in North America. One of them named the place Banff for a county in Scotland. In 1885, after a dispute among commercial interests over exploitation of the resources there, the Canadian Government set aside a ten-square-mile tract at Banff as a national park. It has grown to more than 2,500 square miles in the years since and the hot springs have become one of its lesser attractions. It's no wonder. They have plenty of competition. The park has several peaks more than 10,000 feet high, including 11,870-foot Mount Assiniboine, Banff's highest. It has glaciers and thickly-forested mountain valleys. It has wildly rushing rivers and lakes with water so clean and clear that the mountains are perfectly reflected in them. Among them is Lake Louise. The Indians knew it as the Lake of the Little Fishes, but the railroad surveyors quickly changed it to Emerald Lake. Even more quickly it was renamed to honor the daughter of Queen Victoria who became a Canadian when her husband was appointed Canada's Governor General. Is it the most beautiful lake in the entire world?

Anyone seeing it for the first time framed on two sides by high mountains and on a third by a glacier, all of which is reflected in its blue-green water, would be hard pressed to name a competitor for the title.

If Banff National Park was created to stop destruction of natural beauty by commercial interests, the commercial interests of the Canadian Pacific Railroad made it both accessible and more desirable. When the railroad opened for business in early 1886 it went right to work promoting the trip across the continent as a grand adventure. Their right-of-way crossed the Rockies at an altitude of 5,337 feet, which gave riders a spectacular view. But it also gave the CP's locomotives a tough uphill climb on the westbound trip. What goes up must come down, of course, and the run down the other side of the mountain was a good deal longer and a good bit steeper. At one point, the drop was more than a thousand feet in less than seven miles. The uphill run was easily accomplished by adding a few more locomotives and a lot more patience. But going down the western slope was quite another story. Trains were required to come to a full stop at several different points along the way so their brakes could be inspected, and more often than not they needed to be replaced. It all took time and to make sure their passengers spent the time in solid comfort, the Canadian Pacific built the most luxurious rolling stock of any railroad in the world at the time. The sleeping berths were both longer and wider than those on competing American railroads, which meant that the cars had to be bigger. They were more opulent, too, with hundreds of pounds of solid woodwork and brass fittings both inside and out. It all conspired to put a strain on the locomotives that was relieved in some ways by eliminating dining cars from the trains.

That helped solve the weight problem but it created another. It took five days to make the transcontinental trip if there were no avalanches or mechanical problems, and all that fresh air along the way could make passengers ravenous. Rest stops were the answer, and the CP thoughtfully provided them at strategic points along the way. The railroad was careful to select the most scenic locations for them and passengers were usually reluctant to get back on the train again after dining at one of them. The answer to that problem was even easier. The best of the rest stops became hotels, and among the best of them was the one they called Banff Springs.

The railroad rarely missed a trick, but when the hotel was finished at Banff, it had inadvertedly been built facing the wrong direction. There is not a view in the park that isn't spectacular, but some are better than others and the best outlook from the new hotel was from the back of the ground floor. But that is where the kitchens were. The building couldn't be turned around so they did the next-best thing. They added a pavilion to the back of the building so no one, except possibly the chef, would be disappointed. They didn't make the same mistake when they built the equally fabulous Chateau Lake Louise, also in Banff National Park. It sits dramatically at the head of the amazing lake that gives it its name. Most of its guest rooms and all of its public rooms overlook a wide lawn that sweeps down to the lake shore. From the day the hotel opened, guests there have been encouraged to leave wake-up calls that will allow them to watch the sun come up over Lake Louise, and no one who takes advantage of the service ever regrets it, even though at some times of the year the call can come as early as four in the morning.

The two hotels, both of which are often listed among the world's best, have naturally become reasons for going to Banff, but even without them the natural attractions would be reason enough. Among them are the huge rock pillars named hoodoos by the early trappers, who believed they could bring bad luck. There is no reason to believe they were right. The pillars are simply glacial till, a collection of sand, clay, rocks and gravel left behind by a glacier. Over time they've resisted erosion and become tightly fastened in place by the lime-filled glacial runoff that swirled around them and twisted them into fantastic shapes.

And if Lake Louise is the most beautiful lake in the world, the runners-up are nearby. Mirror Lake and Lake Agnes are among them, so is Lake Minnewanka, the only one in the park that allows motor boats and takes advantage of the fact with sightseeing launches. One of the springs that started it all is in a cave on Sulphur Mountain. It spews out more than 575,000 gallons of hot water a day, feeding a sulphur pool whose year-round temperature is 88 degrees and a freshwater pool that is only a few degrees cooler. Higher up on the mountain, another spring feeds a swimming pool that is warm enough for swimming on the coldest days of winter. Since the 1960s it has had plenty of winter bathers from among the thousands who flock there for the skiing at one of five major ski centers. The slopes of Mount Norquay have a downhill course that drops a breathtaking 2,000 feet, not to mention an Olympic standard ski jump. The skiing season there begins in early November and is still going strong in May. In some areas the snowfall is more than 350 inches a year.

A visit to any of Canada's 28 National Parks is usually a learning experience as well as a return to nature. But at Banff it's possible to get college credit for the experience. In 1933 the University of Calgary set up a campus in the park known as the Banff Center. Its summer session ends each year with the week-long Festival of the Arts. But its two theaters are open year-round for concerts, ballet and dramatic presentations. Students there study the arts, but the Center also offers them courses in photography, French and crafts, among other disciplines. The school also offers courses in business and government and conducts graduate courses in management skills in the School of Advanced Management, sponsored by the Universities of Alberta, Manitoba and Saskatchewan.

Calgary is usually considered the gateway to Banff. Its sister city and arch-rival, Edmonton, is the traditional jumping-off point for trips into the much larger Jasper National Park. But there is no need to get involved in the family feud, which began when the railroad surveyors chose a southerly route through Calgary rather than through Edmonton for its first transcontinental route. The two parks are connected by the Ice-Field Highway, a 142-mile road that follows the Continental Divide past dramatic glaciers and icefields, including the Columbia Ice Field, the biggest accumulation of ice anywhere in the Rockies, covering 110 square miles to a depth of up to a thousand feet.

Jasper covers 4,200 square miles of towering mountains, flower-filled valleys, waterfalls and lakes. Its three main glacier systems feed the Athabasca and Mackenzie Rivers, which flow north toward the Arctic Ocean, the Columbia, which heads west to the Pacific, and the Saskatchewan, which eventually empties into Lake Winnipeg, more than a thousand miles to the east.

The park was established in 1907. It takes its name from a supply post that was established at the mouth of the Rocky River in 1813 by Jasper Hawkes. Much less primitive is the luxurious Jasper Park Lodge. The views from its main building and cottages are nothing short of spectacular, and if a guest prefers to stay inside and look out at it, room service is provided by the hotel's famous bicycle-riding waiters. Those who do stay indoors are missing some wonderful opportunities for hiking, though. They miss the fun of the sky tram that takes visitors up the side of Whistler Mountain at a speed of some 1,400 feet a minute. At the top they could be enjoying skiing in August or just enjoying the view from 7,500 feet up.

Possibly the most unusual of Jasper's natural wonders is Maligne Canyon. In places the Maligne River, which carved its craggy walls from the limestone, vanishes beneath the surface and becomes an underground river. Medicine Lake also feeds the underground system and in the dry season almost disappears in the process.

Hikers in the canyon can often hear the roar of underground waterfalls. But even though the valley has some spectacular waterfalls above ground, one of the highest in all Canada is a good reason to head west into British Columbia for a visit to Yoho National Park, a 507 square-mile preserve that includes Takakkaw Falls, a 1,240-foot-high spectacle of cascading water. Nearby is Laughing Falls which, though a mere 50 feet

high, is also worth the trip to the Yoho River Valley. It is always partially hidden behind a beautiful cloud of mist. The Cree Indians named Yoho. It is their word for "wonderful," and no other word suits it as well. The best way to see the wonders of Yoho is on foot and its gentle valleys make hiking an experience almost anyone can enjoy. But for people who prefer to enjoy nature from the comfort of their cars or through the window of a train, the 133-mile-long Kicking Horse Trail passes through some of the best scenery in the park. The trail is named for Kicking Horse Pass, the park's eastern gateway.

South of Yoho is Kootenay National Park, also easily seen from the highway which follows the valleys of the Vermilion and Kootenay Rivers. The Vermilion was named for the ochre beds that are one of the park's attractions. They are cold mineral springs that bring iron oxide to the surface of the bogs and leave behind deposits of reddish-brown color that contrasts with the rich green moss. The Indians used the color to paint their bodies.

The Blackfoot Indians used a lot of war paint. They had the reputation of being among the fiercest of all the western tribes. Their main hunting ground is now Waterton Lakes National Park, which is connected to the larger United States National Park, Glacier, across the border in Montana, to form the Waterton-Glacier International Peace Park. Waterton Lakes was made a Canadian National Park in 1895 after an oil boom hit southern Alberta. Local civic groups petitioned the government to set aside some of the territory to keep it from being filled with oil wells, and the 200-square-mile park was the result. Waterton's prime attraction is a chain of four long, narrow lakes, one of which reflects the spectacular mountain view for guests of the Prince of Wales Hotel. The mountains that frame the view are among the oldest in all the Rockies and show their age in glorious shades of red and purple, green and gray. But Waterton is more than just rocks. The prairie meets the mountains at the edge of the park and colorful wildflowers bloom from late spring to midsummer across the fields and up the slopes.

The American Glacier National Park adjoining Waterton Lakes is considered one of the most ruggedly beautiful of all the parks in the United States. But Canada's Glacier National Park in the mountains of British Columbia is so rugged that from the time it was established in 1886, its only access was by train until the Trans-Canada Highway was opened in 1962. The park's 521 square miles cover the most incredibly beautiful section of the Selkirk Mountains.

They are snowier than almost any other mountain range in the world, with an annual average of 342 inches. The snow feeds the glaciers, ten of which are in the confines of the park. And when snowfall is greater than the rate of melting, which is often, avalanches follow. The highway that runs for some 30 miles through Glacier would have been a notable engineering feat simply because of the high mountains it had to cross. It reaches 4,400 feet on the side of 9,482-foot-high Mount MacDonald. But the threat of avalanches made it necessary to build elaborate concrete snowsheds and other barriers along the way. And even that isn't enough. Among the equipment park personnel rely on is a cannon that is used to lob artillery shells into threatening snowbanks to create controlled, and therefore less dangerous, avalanches. The dangers of passing through the Selkirks by train were minimized in 1916 by the longest railroad tunnel in North America, the seven-mile Connaught Tunnel. But the train ride is still a great adventure even if part of it is underground.

The adventure continues as the railroad and the new highway progress westward into Mount Revelstoke National Park, named for an 8,000-foot-high peak in the Selkirk Mountains. By Canadian standards, the 100 square-mile park is small, but what it lacks in size it makes up for in spectacle. A gravel road winds for 16 miles up the side of the mountain for one of the best wilderness views anywhere. And the views along the way make it difficult to concentrate on negotiating the hairpin turns.

It's often difficult to concentrate on driving in any national park. Among the things they protect is the wildlife. In Mount Revelstoke, a driver can be distracted by a black bear or a mountain goat or a soaring golden eagle. Less surprising, but just as engrossing, are the herds of elk and moose and mule deer at Elk Island National Park near Edmonton, in Alberta. But what the name doesn't tell is that this is also home to one of the largest herds of bison left in North America. The nature preserve that was established in 1906 acquired a herd of about 700 plains bison which grew by leaps and bounds to some 5,000 animals in less than 15 years. By 1924, fearing that the herd would soon overflow the available grazing land, 2,400 of them were shot. The destruction was stopped within a year and some 6,600 of the bison were herded north to the newly established Wood Buffalo National Park which was home to the last remaining herd of northern woods bison, a close cousin of the variety that once roamed the great plains. Nature took its own course after that. The two species mated with each other, creating a new species and seemingly making the woods bison extinct in the process. The part of the herd that had been left at Elk Island is still made up of purebred plains bison, and in 1957 biologists found a small herd of purebred woods bison, which is now being used as stock to rebuild the species.

Unless you're a biologist, you might not be able to tell the difference between a woods bison and a plains bison. You might even call them both buffaloes. A lot of people do. But seeing the herds running free at Wood Buffalo and Elk Island National Parks is a sight to take your breath away. Or at the very least to take you back in time a century or so to an era when these magnificent beasts made the earth tremble in all parts of western North America.

The parks where the buffalo roam protected haven't changed since the days when Indians hunted there. But there are parks in Canada where time has been standing still since long before any man arrived on the scene. Among them is Kluane National Park in the Yukon Territory. It takes its name, which is pronounced *klu-áh-nee*, from 184-square-mile Kluane Lake. But the huge lake is only one of the park's special features. Within its 8,500 square miles of wilderness is St. Elias Icefield, one of the largest anywhere in the world outside the Arctic, which was there at the beginning of the Ice Age. Kluane borders on Alaska and is very near to the Pacific Ocean, whose moisture is carried inland and stopped by the high mountains. The precipitation keeps the icefield intact, just as it has for thousands of years. The St. Elias Mountains, which run through the park, are the highest in Canada, with a dozen peaks more than 15,000 feet high, including 19,525-foot-high Mt. Logan, the highest peak in the country.

The Alaska Highway passes Kluane's northeastern boundary for some 80 miles, making it relatively easy to reach. Nahanni National Park in the Northwest Territories is quite another story. The only way to get there is by plane, or by canoe for people who are expert at handling one. But for a place to get away from the madding crowd, there are few places in the world quite like it. It takes its name from a race of fierce giants the Indians say once lived there. They called them Nahannis, "the people far away," and even the most warlike of tribes preferred to keep far away from them. In our enlightened times, we write off such things as primitive legends. But in fact, in

1908 the McCleod brothers went into the area in search of gold and may have encountered the reality of the tales the Indians told. Almost no white men had ever been where they went, but they were experienced in the ways of the wilderness and decided to spend the winter there. In the spring another prospector found their dead bodies in what is now called Deadmen Valley. The mountains behind it are known as the Headless Range because the bodies were found without their heads. The Mounted Police began an investigation and, though the Mounties are famous for always getting their man, to this day the book is still open on the case. Were the McCleods victims of fierce giants? No one knows. But no one knows they weren't, either.

Today it is giving new meaning to the thrill of white water rafting for adventuresome visitors. But not many people had the courage to follow the McCleods up the South Nahanni River until the magnificent 1,840-square-mile wilderness was established as a national park in 1972 to save it from being converted into a source for hydro-electric power. The power resources would have been awesome. The river roars over a 294-foot-high waterfall after racing wildly through three dramatic canyons. The power of the water going over Virginia Falls makes the ground tremble and its roar can be heard for miles. If the falls are the climax, getting to them is one of nature's great spectacles. The walls of First Canyon are a sheer 3,500 feet high and pitted with caves. The other two are slightly less high, but no less wonderful. At the end of the third, the river is forced through an abrupt hairpin turn, and after another forty miles it crashes through Hell's Gate, a sudden wall of rock that sends it racing though a figure-eight pattern before it straightens out again near the brink of the falls.

Though its growing season is quite short, hot springs have created luxurious vegetation in many parts of Nahanni. But there are no such amenities in the 8,300-square-mile Auyuittuq, the only National Park north of the Arctic Circle. Its name, which comes from the Inuit language, means "the place which does not melt." The word, which doesn't exactly melt off the tongue, is pronounced *ah-you-i-tuck*. When the park was established in 1972, it was called Baffin Island National Park. But in 1979, reasoning that the name didn't do justice to the place or to the Inuit people who have lived there for thousands of years, Parks Canada decided a change was in order.

If spelling or pronouncing its name is difficult, getting there is harder still. There is a scheduled airline service to Frobisher Bay from Montreal and it's usually possible to get a flight from there across Cumberland Sound to Pangnirtung. The entrance to the park is another 20 miles from there up at the end of the fiord. Sometimes it's possible to make the trip by canoe, but the ice doesn't break up until well into July and it freezes again in a few weeks. It's also possible to rent a snowmobile at Pangnirtung, but many visitors prefer to make the trip on foot. Some others charter small planes and secure special permission to fly into Auyuittuq. But once anyone is in the park they usually get around under their own power. Camping is permitted in designated places, but in all that territory, which is bigger than the State of Israel, there are fewer than 20 individual campsites.

The wind almost never stops blowing at Auyuittuq. Sometimes it roars at hurricane force for days on end. The heat of the summer is never higher than 50 degrees Fahrenheit and in winter the temperature drops to well below zero and stays there. From May until July the sun shines 24 hours a day, but in the winter it doesn't shine at all. There are no trees, except for occasional groves of stunted willows, but in June and July carpets of bright-colored wildflowers thrive. If it is a hostile environment Auyuittuq's incredible beauty more than makes up for it. The mountains soar some 7,000 feet into the air, in places cliffs rise 3,000 feet straight up from the sea. And it is, indeed, "the place which does not melt." The Penny Ice Cap at the top of the mountains covers 2,200 square miles and at least one glacier extending down from it is 20 miles long and two miles wide.

And though Auyuittuq is certainly not overrun with tourists, it is not impossible to explore and there are few adventures in the world that compare to it. The best way to experience the park is by charter airplane, usually available from Frobisher Bay. The pilots are experienced and fly their clients to the best places for fishing and sightseeing and to Inuit villages, where overnight accommodations are available. The opportunity to meet and talk with the Inuit people is one of the best reasons for making the trip. It's a trip that needs to be coordinated long in advance, however, and it can be an expensive one. But the anticipation alone is one of the pleasures.

Auyuittuq is on a fiord-laced peninsula overlooking Baffin Bay, which is a favorite haunt of polar bears, whales, walruses and seals. A continent away at Pacific Rim National Park on the west side of British Columbia's Vancouver Island, watching whales and seals is a much more comfortable experience, if one doesn't mind rain and fog.

Pacific Rim, which extends for 65 miles along the Pacific coast, is actually three parks in one, each with its own distinct personality. Long Beach is a favorite spot for sea lions who like to take the sun on the hard-packed sand, which is a half mile wide at low tide. Behind the beach is the 4,000-foot-high Mackenzie Mountain Range, and trails lead from the ocean into its forests and around its lakes. The frequent rains and relatively mild climate have produced forests of huge, lush trees and the West Coast Trail section of the park offers a perfect way to experience them on sections of a 45-mile coastal pathway. The trail was originally established in the 19th century so that shipwrecked sailors could find their way back to civilization, and it served its purpose hundreds of times. The usually fog-shrouded Barkley Sound, which cuts into the center of the park, has been the scene of more shipwrecks than any comparable place between Canada and Japan. The Broken Group Islands, the third section of Pacific Rim, is the reason. Though it is still dangerous to navigate through the shoals and among the rocky islands, it is possible to visit them and to find campsites on a half-dozen of them. But many of them are barely big enough to provide space for a sea lion or two to stretch out.

The rocky headlands of Pacific Rim are mirrored at Terra Nova National Park on the eastern edge of Newfoundland. But there is no mistaking one for the other. The Atlantic Ocean pounds Terra Nova's high rocks and icebergs float majestically by. The sea rushes inland through a series of fiords, but it is also a land of gently rolling mountains with virgin forests, bogs and marshes, fast-moving streams and deep, protected coves. In some places it is possible to see as many as six different lakes, each at a different altitude. And the bogs are home to the insect-eating pitcher plant, which has been made the official flower of Newfoundland. The plant thrives in nitrate-poor swampy soils by trapping insects and drowning them in a fluid that also decomposes them and converts them to nutrients.

Terra Nova covers some 154 square miles, and overlooks the cod-rich waters that brought fishermen to North America from Spain and Portugal, Britain and France long before any of them ever thought about staying. On the opposite side of the island, across the spectacular Long Range Mountains, is 750-square-mile Gros Morne National Park. It is named for the 2,644-foot-high mountain that rises majestically in the midst of its 40-mile-long coastline along the Gulf of Saint Lawrence. The salt water fishing there is legendary, but its mountain streams are just as famous for trout and salmon fishing. It's a paradise for sightseeing, too. In some places the mountains rise abruptly from the sea as high as 2,000 feet.

The oldest European settlements in Canada are in the Province of Newfoundland. Vikings who landed there in the first century called it the "Land of Forest." John Cabot, sailing from England in 1497, landed at Cape Bona Vista, near the site of Terra Nova, and renamed it New Founde Isle. He also, coincidentally, named it a British possession. In 1583, Sir Humphrey Gilbert established a town at St. John's, the first British colony in North America. The French, meanwhile, asserted themselves on the western side of Newfoundland when Jacques Cartier sailed into the Strait of Belle Isle at the island's northwest corner in 1534. It was he who first saw the Long Range Mountains and named the Gros Morne. He also claimed what he saw in the name of the King of France and then turned his attention further westward.

Though he had been impressed by the mountains and the shoreline, Cartier was even more impressed by the abundance of fish he saw there. The British, who also knew the commercial value of codfish, disputed his claim on the grounds that Cabot had been there first. The matter was settled in 1783 by the treaty of Versailles, which said that fishing on the west coast of Nova Scotia was open to the French. Lawyers in London interpreted the agreement to mean that the English would share the bounty with the French. But the interpretation in Paris was that the agreement didn't say a thing about sharing. They argued back and forth about it for more than 120 years, finally settling the dispute in 1904, when Britain agreed to give France territory in West Africa in exchange for French fishing rights off Newfoundland.

The result of it all was to delay settlement of the island's west coast and to keep much of it relatively wild to this day. The island across the Gulf of St. Lawrence, Prince Edward Island, was also involved in the feuds between the British and the French, but the British prevailed in 1758 when they occupied the place the French called Ile St-Jean. They began right away to make it safe for their kind of civilization by evicting the French settlers who called themselves

Acadians. Then they divided it into 67 farms of 20,000 acres each and held a lottery in London to sell them to the highest bidders. It took the farmers who worked the land and paid huge rents for the privilege until 1873 to earn the right to buy back the land from their absentee landlords, but during all that time they kept right on farming. The result is a rather civilized place, but a 25-mile stretch of beach along the island's north shore is kept forever wild in Prince Edward Island National Park. The beach is one of the best in all Canada, backed by gentle sand dunes and high red sandstone cliffs. The sand on most of the beaches and the soil all over the island, for that matter, is a rich, reddish-brown color because of the high iron content of the soil, which causes it to "rust" when it's exposed to the air. But there is more to the park than salt water and colorful beaches. The fresh water streams and ponds attract some 200 species of birds, including the great blue heron.

If a green-winged teal or a ring-necked duck should decide to fly out to the Atlantic Ocean from Prince Edward Island, its next landfall would be Cape Breton Highlands on the northern tip of Nova Scotia's Cape Breton Island. It's a short trip as the duck flies, but by car it's close to 300 miles and includes a 75-minute ferryboat ride. But the last part of the trip is along the Cabot Trail, a 172-mile-long highway loop that skirts the edge of Cape Breton.

It is one of the most beautiful automobile trips on the east coast of North America. And it leads through a world that could easily have been plucked from the Scottish Highlands and set down here between the Gulf of Saint Lawrence and the Atlantic Ocean. The people, many of whom prefer Gaelic as their first language, add to the other world flavor, though in many places the descendants of Acadians who escaped deportation in the mid-18th century manage to keep their French culture alive there, too.

But the people only add to the pleasure, just as the 367 square-mile Cape Breton Highlands National Park adds to the pleasure of the Cabot Trail. The road winds for 70 miles through the park along its western, northern and eastern boundaries. It goes over four mountain peaks ranging from 1,200 to 1,500 feet within the park, but Cape Breton's highest point, 1,747-foot-high White Hill, is almost at the geographic

center of the park in a section known as the Everlasting Barren. The moors that cover the plateau occupy about 90 percent of Cape Breton Highlands and are laced with rivers and creeks, gorges and deep valleys.

The two-lane highway enters the park from the southwest at Ingonish Beach, a wide stretch of sand at the foot of a 1,200-foot-high mountain known as Cape Smoky because of the mist that almost always hides its summit. It also passes near another reminder of Scotland, the Highlands Golf Course, which has some natural water hazards that would make native Scots green with envy and gives park visitors challenges they don't soon forget. After the Cabot Trail leaves the park near Pleasant Bay, it winds its way over high mountains and along the wild coast overlooking the Gulf of St. Lawrence. It is a beautiful drive any time of the year, but experienced travelers say the best time is around the first two weeks in October, the most likely time to see the fall colors, which combine beautifully with the seascape.

Cape Breton has been a part of Nova Scotia for more than a century, but the people there seem to prefer not to notice. They like things the way they were and continue to cling to their old customs and languages. But well over 5,000 of the people of Nova Scotia are Micmac Indians, and though they have long since abandoned some of their old customs, their language lives on in place names like that of Kejimkujik National Park. The name, pronounced *ke-jim-kóo-jik*, comes from the largest of a dozen lakes within its 238 square miles. It was once a Micmac Indian reservation, but became a national park in 1968.

When the British took over Nova Scotia in 1755, the French Acadians were driven out, but the Micmacs, who had seen Europeans come and go since as early as 1518, adapted quite easily to the new form of "civilization." They had long since adopted the white man's religion and had begun dressing like the people who had come among them. But long before that their ancestors had hunted deer in the evergreen forests of Kejimkujik, had guided their canoes over its lakes and trapped beaver and mink along its streams. They recorded their triumphs by scratching pictures in the rocks with stones and beaver teeth, later using the white man's iron tools. But though civilization changed them, it hardly touched Kejimkujik.

Kejimkujik is part of what the poet Longfellow called "the forest primeval" in his tale of the expulsion of the Acadians. But much of the territory had been turned into farmland long before the British came. The original French Acadia extended across the Bay of Fundy into what is now the Province of New Brunswick. And though some of the oldest settlements in Canada are along its rivers and seacoast, nearly 90 percent of the province is still forested land, just as it was when the French explorer Champlain traded with the Micmacs there back in 1534.

A dense forest home of moose and deer, black bears and lynx covers most of the 80 square miles of Fundy National Park, but the bluffs and crags of its eight-mile shoreline are the park's main attraction for most visitors. The tidal flats there are a treasure house of small marine life and shells, but twice a day strollers at the water's edge find the water edging them out. The highest tides anywhere in the world are at the eastern end of the Bay of Fundy. In some places the water has been known to rise as high as 52 feet. According to scientists, about one hundred billion tons of water rushes in from the Atlantic Ocean to the narrow bay every 12 hours and 30 minutes. It is, they say, equal to the flow of all the rivers in the world in a full 24 hours. Off Fundy National Park, the tide creeps rather than roars in. People walking the beach begin to notice water lapping their ankles where they had been digging their toes into the mud. In about half an hour, if they don't move inland, it will be waist high, within six hours the water will be more than 40 feet deep. Then the tide turns and in another six hours the same strollers will be leaving footprints in the soft mud again.

For those who prefer not to play in the mud but enjoy salt water, the park has a swimming pool filled with water piped up from the bay and thoughtfully heated. There is a golf course there, too, and tennis courts and two amphitheaters where outdoor performances help add to Fundy's charm as an excellent, civilized place for family vacations. But there are forest trails, hidden valleys, streams, flowers and wildlife enough to satisfy anyone's longing for outdoor adventure.

There is no heated swimming pool at nearby Kouchibouguac National Park on New Brunswick's southeast shore. But its beaches that stretch for 16 miles along the shore of the Gulf of St. Lawrence rival any stretch of beach all the way down the east coast to the Florida Keys. The Micmacs are responsible for the name, which is pronounced *koo-chi-boo-ack* and means

"river of the long tides." Though the tides are tiny compared to Fundy, they leave their impression in the waterways, lagoons and salt marshes behind the dunes, creeping far inland teeming with tiny marine life and then quietly receding, leaving the living treasure behind. The people who live near there say that every major storm along the east coast brings some change to the beaches of Kouchibouguac, but they are well-protected by the dunes behind them and by a chain of offshore sandy islands.

But there is more to the park than beaches. It is a major rest stop for migrating birds and the park has one of North America's biggest colonies of terns. Seals enjoy visiting Kouchibouguac, too, and the forests shelter moose and deer, black bears and beaver. The inland bogs are estimated to be more than 10,000 years old and nurture a wide variety of shrubs and mosses and no less than 25 different species of orchids.

In Forillon National Park, at the tip of Quebec's Gaspé Peninsula, most of the beaches are accessible only at low tide. Like Kouchibouguac, it overlooks the Gulf of St. Lawrence, but the similarity ends there. Forillon covers 92 square miles of rugged cliffs rising straight up from the water and capped with a crown of thick forests and flower-strewn meadows. The park, which was established in 1970, gets its name from the French word for a small lighthouse. The first settlers there built bonfires on a rock that has long since been reclaimed by the sea as a landmark for fishermen. Though men have been harvesting huge quantities of fish from the waters off Forillon for more than 400 years, there are still plenty of them out there. No creatures know that better than the hundreds of seals who have taken up residence on the flat offshore rocks, or the huge whales who arrive in the early spring and stay until late fall feasting on the small fish.

Human visitors to Forillon find the fishing terrific, too. But, unlike the whales, they aren't limited to the salt water variety. Forillon has five freshwater lakes and several rivers and streams, all of which are teeming with fish.

Forillon is a paradise for birdwatchers, too, and there are many miles of hiking trails to get to where the birds are, and possibly to watch a moose or a deer along the way. The park is the permanent home of thousands of gulls and cormorants, but in spring and summer it is visited by more than 200 different species of birds.

The Chick-Chock Mountains in the center of the Gaspé Peninsula are the highest in eastern Canada and have kept settlers from building towns anywhere but along the coast, and to this day comparatively few people live in inland Gaspé. But nearly half the population of Quebec, Canada's biggest province, lives a short distance down the St. Lawrence River in Montreal and its suburbs. And more than a half million others live nearby in Quebec City.

When they want to get away from it all, they usually head for the Laurentian Highlands and a national park about midway between the two cities, La Mauricie, a 211-square-mile reserve in the valley of the St. Maurice River. The park has so many lakes, no one has gotten around to naming some of them. It is laced with waterfalls because it straddles the boundary between the mountains and the St. Lawrence lowlands, a dividing line that gives the park a combination of evergreen and hardwood forests. Cataracts notwithstanding, La Mauricie is a paradise for canoeists, who can paddle their way into deep forests that haven't changed at all since French trappers ran their lines through the same hills, which are estimated to have been there for more than 600 million years, making them the oldest mountains in the world.

The entrance to La Mauricie is on a road that winds its way through beautifully-scenic farm country and passes near some of the best-developed resorts in Canada. Provincial parks nearby add to the untouched wildness of the area even though it is within easy distance of two major cities. There are cities and towns all along the banks of the St. Lawrence, and near the point where the river flows out of Lake Ontario, not far from the industrial city of Kingston, Ontario, is the thousand-acre St. Lawrence Islands National Park. It is Canada's smallest, but is no less wild and rugged than many of the others. It is made up of nearly 100 islands, less than 20 of which support any plant life, and only one of which is accessible by road, though the others can be reached by boat or water taxi. The park's headquarters, a beach and campsites are on the mainland overlooking the rocky islands, which were formed more than 500 million years ago in an upheaval of granite, known to geologists as the Frontenac Axis, that forms the boundary between the Canadian Shield and the Adirondack Mountains. The islands forested with pines, shrubs and white oaks are composed of the same granite and limestone as all the others,

but a thin layer of soil and the height of the rocks above the water makes their crowns of green possible. Unlike most of Canada's national parks, St. Lawrence Islands doesn't have a population of big mammals, but it is a favorite haunt of ducks and gulls, herons and other water fowl.

The Canadian Shield, which begins at the St. Lawrence, covers more than 2 million square miles of eastern and central Canada. Among the best places to study its effects on the landscape is the largest national park in Ontario, the 725 square-mile Pukaskwa on a 50-mile stretch of the north shore of Lake Superior. The park, whose name is pronounced *púk-a-saw*, is still being developed and its wildness is far from tamed. It can't be reached by road but visitors often arrive there in power boats and then walk or paddle canoes into the interior. It is almost guaranteed that no visitor will see another human at any point during the adventure. Instead they will hear the lonely call of loons in the distance and will see caribou and moose and any one of more than 200 species of birds. Pukaskwa is also a good place to study arctic and alpine plants, which thrive there because of the cooling effect of the great inland sea the park borders.

Another of the Great Lakes, Lake Erie, surrounds Ontario's Point Pelee National Park on three sides. It fills six miles of the tip of a long sandy peninsula. Point Pelee is completely different from any of the other national parks of Canada. It is the southernmost point of the country and has a long, frost-free growing season which encourages lush vegetation in the spring and almost desert-like conditions in the heat of midsummer. Point Pelee has varieties of trees that don't grow in other parts of Canada and many are festooned with vines that give parts of the park an almost jungle-like quality. Two thirds of Point Pelee is filled with freshwater marshes which produce an abundance of insects in the spring. Though they can make life unpleasant for a few weeks, they give the park its major attraction for visitors and naturalists alike. More than 90 species of birds have made the peninsula their permanent home and, because it is located on two different migratory flyways, it is a favorite stopping place for another 330 species in the spring and fall. The 5,000-foot-long boardwalk that spans the marshes, and other well-marked viewing places, including a 20-foot observation tower, makes watching the birds relatively easy, but everywhere in the park listening to their songs is an unforgettable delight.

The most unforgettable experience Point Pelee offers is in September, when thousands of colorful monarch butterflies arrive to put on their show. Because it is one of the most heavily used of all of Canada's national parks, automobile traffic into it has been restricted. A transit system called the Tip takes visitors into the park in quiet, pollution-free trackless trains which include an interpretive talk along the way. And moments of silence to allow visitors to listen to the birds.

Ontario's Georgian Bay Islands National Park in Lake Huron is reached, as the name implies, by boat. There are some 3,000 islands in the area, 50 of which form the park. They have a wild beauty that was made famous by a group of seven painters who formed a loose organization they called the Group of Seven and concentrated on painting the fantastic rock formations and wind-twisted trees which make the islands unique. Beausoleil Island, which is, at 4.2 square miles, bigger than all the other islands in the park combined, is reached by boat from Honey Harbour and has facilities for camping and hiking and swimming. Flowerpot Island, the second-largest with 495 acres, is located 100 miles away to the northwest and is reached by boat from Tobermory. It was named for two rock formations that are 35 and 50 feet high and resemble giant flowerpots. Nature has added to the symbolism by scattering flowers and shrubs among their crevices. Nature has also been at work destroying them through the action of wind and water. They have been preserved and protected with man-made waterproofing and masonry.

The islands and the sky are reflected in the clear blue water, and Georgian Bay Islands is a favorite place for scuba divers to explore the wrecks of ships that didn't manage to clear the rocks. Scuba diving is a rare sport in Canada. In most places the only creatures intrepid enough for it are beavers, and among the places visitors are most likely to see them at work is at Riding Mountain National Park in western Manitoba. The park is located along the Manitoba escarpment, a thousand-mile ridge that rises from the plains across Saskatchewan, Manitoba and North Dakota. Riding Mountain itself is 2,480 feet high overlooking the 1,150-square-mile park that includes three different natural habitats. The mountains are covered with pine forests that give way at lower elevations to hardwoods and ferns. In the western part of the park, huge areas are meadows and grasslands covered with wildflowers in the spring and early summer. The wildlife there is as varied as the landscape. It was where buffalo once roamed free and

Riding Mountain has a herd of bison contained within a 2,000-acre enclosure of meadows and woods. The park also has one of the biggest elk herds in Canada. But it's the fish that lure the most visitors. The creatures come in record sizes at Riding Mountain. Northern pike with a fighting weight of as many as 30 pounds have been pulled from Clear Lake, and the rainbow trout and walleyes in other nearby lakes are just as legendary.

Canada's famous conservationist and writer Grey Owl lived in a cabin near Beaver Lake at Riding Mountain, but in the last few years of his life he moved west into Saskatchewan and lived on the shores of Lake Ajawaan in Prince Albert National Park, where he is buried today. Grey Owl spent much of his life in the wilderness conducting a passionate campaign to stop the killing of animals for sport. His appearance and his beliefs about the natural way of things led most of his followers to think he was an Indian. In fact, many of the Indians he came in contact with accepted him as their brother. But just before his death in 1938 he revealed that he had been born in England and had come to Canada as a boy. It didn't really matter to anyone. He certainly wasn't the only Canadian of his time who hadn't been born there and he touched the souls of enough other Canadians to make a difference in their level of respect for their fellow creatures who shared their land.

Prince Albert National Park, where he chose to spend his last years, is an entirely fitting setting for such a man. The 1,150-square-mile preserve has prairies, rolling hills, high mountains, lakes, streams and valleys and wildlife ranging from bison to black bear, caribou and elk. The park also has a huge colony of white pelicans and an abundance of beavers, the animal Grey Owl worked hardest to save.

Parks Canada has been at work since the establishment of the national park at Banff in 1885 to save the natural landscape of Canada. The agency has identified 48 distinct natural regions for conservation and, though it has succeeded in placing at least one national park in each province and territory of the country, it has not yet finished the challenge of having each natural region represented. When Grasslands National Park opens in Saskatchewan, there will be 29 parks in the system and yet another region will be represented in the form of prairie land that was once home to millions of bison and a major hunting ground of the Sioux Indians. It will include historic Frenchman Creek and a piece of the so-called "badlands," in which sandstone hills are still being thrust up from the earth. Grasslands is a place of hot summers, cold winters and very little precipitation. It supports rare grasses and animals found nowhere else in Canada, including prairie dogs and some species of hawks that have adapted themselves to this unusual environment. Grasslands is also a place where the pronghorn antelopes love to play and where thousands of visitors will find an exhilarating pleasure watching them.

Eventually still other parks will be established, and in the future the Canada that was will be among the treasures of the Canada to be. As the history of the land itself goes, we haven't been here very long. It is sobering to think that Sandford Fleming's expedition to find a route for a transcontinental railroad was in 1872, little more than a century ago. When he finally went back east, he wrote:

"Looking back over the vast breadth of the Dominion when our journeyings were ended, it rolled out before us like a panorama, varied and magnificent enough to stir the dullest spirit into patriotic emotion.... From the sea pastures and coal fields of Nova Scotia; from historic Louisburg up the St. Lawrence to historic Quebec; through the great Province of Ontario and on lakes that are seas ... on the chain of lakes where the Ojibway is at home in his canoe, to the plains where the Cree is equally at home on his horse; through the prairie Province of Manitoba and the rolling meadows and park-like country out of which a dozens Manitobas will be carved; along the banks of rivers full-fed by the exhaustless glaciers of the Rocky Mountains ... on to the mountains which will open their gates more widely than to our wealthier neighbors and lead us to the Pacific, down deep gorges filled with timber, beside rivers whose ancient deposits are gold beds and channels choked with fish.... Over all this we had traveled and it was all our own."

Fleming's experience and his feelings are easily recreated today thanks to the 28 national parks that stretch across Canada like stars in a constellation.

Parks Canada, the division of Environment Canada that administers Canada's National Parks, can provide detailed information about facilities in any of them. Ask them by calling (819) 997-2800. Or write to them: Parks Canada, Ottawa, Ontario K1A 1G2. In addition, every park has its own office and superintendent. For more specific information, use this list:

AUYUITTUQ NATIONAL PARK
Pangnirtung, Northwest Territories X0A 0R0
Telephone: (819) 437-8962
Open mid-May to mid-September

BANFF NATIONAL PARK
Box 900, Banff, Alberta T0L 0C0
Telephone: (403) 762-3324
Open all year

CAPE BRETON HIGHLANDS NATIONAL PARK
Ingonish Beach, Cape Breton, Nova Scotia B0C 1L0
Telephone: (902) 285-2270
Some sections open all year

ELK ISLAND NATIONAL PARK
Site 4, R.R.1, Fort Saskatchewan, Alberta T8L 2N7
Telephone: (403) 998-3781
Open all year, but with seasonal services

FORILLON NATIONAL PARK
Box 1220, Gaspé, Quebec G0C 1R0
Telephone: (418) 368-5505
Some sections open all year

FUNDY NATIONAL PARK
Alma, New Brunswick E0A 1B0
Telephone: (506) 887-2000
Some sections open all year

GEORGIAN BAY ISLANDS NATIONAL PARK
Box 28, Honey Harbour, Ontario P0E 1E0
Telephone (705) 756-2415
Open all year

GLACIER NATIONAL PARK
Box 350, Revelstoke, British Columbia V0E 2S0
Telephone: (604) 837-5155
Some sections open all year

GROS MORNE NATIONAL PARK
Box 130, Rocky Harbour, Bonne Bay, Newfoundland A0K 4N0
Telephone: (709) 458-2417
Some sections open all year

JASPER NATIONAL PARK
Box 10, Jasper, Alberta T0E 10E
Telephone: (403) 852-4401
Open all year, limited facilities in winter

KEJIMKUJIK NATIONAL PARK
Box 36, Maitland Bridge, Annapolis County, Nova Scotia B0T 1N0
Telephone: (902) 242-2770
Some sections open all year

KLUANE NATIONAL PARK
Haines Junction, Yukon Territory Y0B 1L0
Telephone: (403) 634-2251
Some sections open all year

KOOTENAY NATIONAL PARK
Box 220, Radium Hot Springs, British Columbia V0A 1M0
Telephone: (604) 347-9615
Some sections open all year

KOUCHIBOUGUAC NATIONAL PARK
Kouchibouguac, Kent County, New Brunswick E0A 2A0
Telephone: (506) 876-2443
Some sections open all year

LA MAURICIE NATIONAL PARK
Box 758, Shawinigan, Quebec G9N 6V9
Telephone: (819) 536-2638
Some sections open all year

MOUNT REVELSTOKE NATIONAL PARK
Box 350, Revelstoke, British Columbia V0E 2S0
Telephone: (604) 837- 5155
Some sections open all year

NAHANNI NATIONAL PARK
Postal Bag 300, Fort Simpson, Northwest Territories X0E 0N0
Telephone: (403) 695-3151
Call for seasonal accessibility

PACIFIC RIM NATIONAL PARK
Box 280, Ucluelet, British Columbia V0R 3A0
Telephone: (604) 726-7721
Open all year

POINT PELEE NATIONAL PARK
R.R. 1, Leamington, Ontario N8H 3V4
Telephone: (519) 326-3204
Open all year

PRINCE ALBERT NATIONAL PARK
Box 100, Waskesiu Lake, Saskatchewan S0J 2Y0
Telephone: (306) 663-5322
Some sections open all year

PRINCE EDWARD ISLAND NATIONAL PARK
Box 487, Charlottetown, Prince Edward Island C1A 7L1
Telephone: (902) 672-2211
Some sections open all year

RIDING MOUNTAIN NATIONAL PARK
Wasagaming, Manitoba R0J 2H0
Telephone: (204) 848-2811
Some sections open all year

ST. LAWRENCE ISLANDS NATIONAL PARK
Box 469, R.R. 3, Mallorytown Landing, Ontario K0E 1R0
Telephone: (613) 923-5241
Open mid-May to mid-October

TERRA NOVA NATIONAL PARK
Glovertown, Newfoundland A0G 2L0
Telephone: (709) 533-2801
Some sections open all year

WATERTON LAKES NATIONAL PARK
Waterton Park, Alberta T0K 2N0
Telephone: (403) 859-2262
Some sections open all year

WOOD BUFFALO NATIONAL PARK
Box 750, Fort Smith, Northwest Territories X0E 0P0
Telephone: (403) 872-2349
Some sections open all year

YOHO NATIONAL PARK
Box 99, Field, British Columbia V0A 1G0
Telephone: (604) 343-6324
Open all year, with limited facilities in winter

AUYUITTUQ

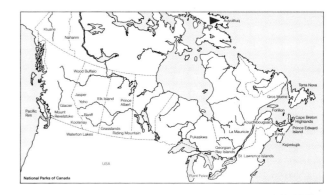

Auyuittuq is a unique arctic wilderness of perpetual ice, mountain peaks and deep valleys on Baffin Island, in Canada's far north.

The need for a quiet, natural, challenging place is common to many people living in the modern world, and this is what draws visitors from all over the world to Auyuittuq.

Above: an emergency cabin at the base of Overlord Peak, Pangnirtung Pass.

Top right: hiking in Weasel River Valley.

Right: a break, simply to wonder at the scenery, during a hike.

Facing page: Glacier hiking at the summit of Pangnirtung Pass, with flat-topped Mount Asgard in the distance.

BANFF

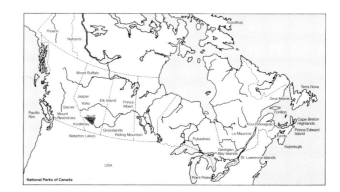

Two views in Banff, the oldest of Canada's national parks.
Left: **Peyto Lake from Lookout Point and** *above* **Lower Waterfowl Lake with Mount Chephren in the background.**

The early light of dawn in Banff National Park as Bow Lake is seen *above* with Portal Peak, Bow Glacier and Mount Thompson in the background. At the other end of the day Mount Rundle *facing page* is reflected in the waters of Vermilion Lake.

Early-morning sunlight on Lake Louise *left and right* **with Victoria Glacier in the background.** *Top:* **Banff Avenue seen from the gardens of the park administration building with Cascade Mountain beyond. St. Nicholas Peak stands high behind the Crowfoot Glacier** *above.*

Above: glacial landscapes, lakes, mountains and clear, clean air all contribute to the magic of Banff National Park. *Facing page:* fresh snow covers the land at Banff's Big Beehive.

CAPE BRETON HIGHLANDS

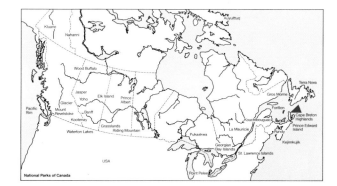

The western shore of Cape Breton Highlands National Park, *left*, looking towards Chéticamp from French Mountain Lookout.
The Cabot Trail – seen *above* as it leads from the Western Shore to French Mountain – takes the traveler right onto the plateau, offering a glimpse of some of the last remaining wilderness in the area.

Facing page: **the delightful Corner Brook, on the trail to Corner Brook Falls.**
Top left: **on the eastern coast, the view towards Middle Head from the Franey
Tower Lookout Point, and** *top right,* **the Atlantic meeting the coast at Green
Cove.** *Above:* **the cliffs and beach at Rocky Bay, north of Broad Cove and**
bottom left, **looking south along the western shore towards Chéticamp from
near Les Grands Falaises.**

ELK ISLAND

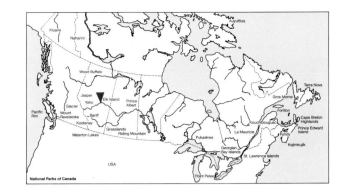

**Frost crisps the grasses and reeds, and early-morning mist
drifts over the surface of Astotin Lake** *left and above.*

A delicate tracery of trees and grasses silhouetted against
the evening sky over Astotin Lake.

Elk Island is a virtual oasis of wilderness in a region dominated by man's civilization. The moods, as seen in these pages, can change rapidly, from misted landscape to glowing sunlight.

From near 'The Point' dawn
sets the sky alight with its
golds and pinks *far right*
across Astotin Lake while
right and bottom right **the
setting sun lays its path on
the lake's waters and
trembling aspens are
reflected in its surface** *facing
page.*
Below: **Canada geese stand
on newly formed ice on
Astotin Lake.**

In addition to the commoner plains bison *bottom right* rare woods bison *below, bottom and facing page* are kept in a separate enclosure south of Highway 16 in Elk Island National Park.

The bull elk and his harem of cows *right* stand in an aspen-bordered glen. Autumn is the rutting, or breeding season for these large members of the deer family.

The bones of a long-dead elk, *top left,* lie in the snow while a muskrat, *top right,* perches on a tree by the water's edge. Trembling aspens reach into the light, *top center,* and fallen trees lie at the eastern boundary of the park *above and above right. Facing page:* snow-spattered trees in the boreal forest in the park's woods bison area.

FORILLON

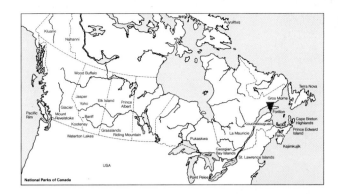

Like a bridal veil, a stream spills its waters over a rock ledge *above* **on the La Chute trail.** *Left:* **flowers of the Arctic Alpine saxifrage.**

The massive, tilted block that forms Forillon contains ten different geological formations dating from the Ordivician to the Devonian period. The pictures on these pages all show varying features of Cap Gaspé with Cap Bon Ami *top right.*

FUNDY

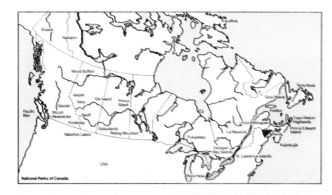

Surrounded by thick forestation, the quiet roadside pond
left **lies near Kinnie Brook, while** *above* **is the energetically-rushing water of Dickson Falls after heavy rain.**

Over 200 species of birds are recorded in Fundy, including the magnificent peregrine falcon *above*. Rising and falling twice each day, the Bay of Fundy's tides are among the highest in the world. Low tide exposes the mud of the Upper Salmon River *top right* and Alma's Beach *far right*. *Right* is the covered bridge over the Forty-Five River and *facing page* Point Wolfe Dam and the covered bridge over the Point Wolfe River.

GEORGIAN BAY ISLANDS

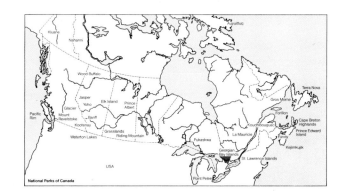

The sun filters through the overhanging branches and foliage to create a lovely woodland scene *left* on Beausoleil Island, the largest in the system. *Above:* the scene at Finger Point.

Top left: the view from Castle Bluff along the north shore of Flowerpot Island. Above Castle Bluff are the caves and rock formations *top right. Left:* "Large Flowerpot" on Flowerpot Island, where the bunchberry *above* and the one-leaf rein orchis *top center* are also found. *Facing page:* the quiet, leaf-covered trail through the woods, near Castle Bluff, Flowerpot Island.

GLACIER

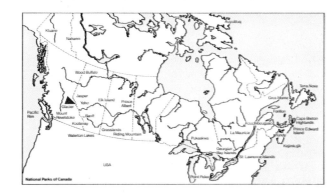

Glacier National Park is located in one of the most rugged areas of
Western Canada – the Selkirk Mountains. *Left* is the view from Alpine
Meadow, on Abbott Ridge, looking towards the Asulkan Glacier and
Dome Point.
　Above: Rogers Pass and the Hermit Range, from Abbott Ridge Trail.

Black bears come in shades that range from black to brown and cinnamon; *right*, this one, a deep cinnamon, has just finished eating leftovers from a plate. Feeding bears and other animals in all of Canada's national parks is strictly forbidden!

The falls *below* are fed by melt waters of the Vaux Glacier (at top of picture) hanging from the slopes of Mount Sir Donald.

Spruce trees, Lookout Mountain and the Asulkan Glacier seen from Glacier Crest, *below far right*.

Left: A hoary marmot takes his ease in Illecillewaet Campground.

Facing page: Clouds move through an alpine valley on the slopes of Mount Sir Donald.

Below: **Western anemone and** *bottom* **bunchberries on the path to Mount Macdonald.** *(Anemone photograph: Parks Canada – J. Belisle).*

The foaming waters of Bear Falls, on Connaught Creek *right* **and,** *facing page,* **Mount Afton at sunset, seen from Glacier Crest.**

GRASSLANDS

A gravel road in Grasslands, *left,* **in the grip of early winter snow.** *Above:* **the folded landscape of the prairie seen from Lookout Point.**

Prairie dogs in the vastness of the prairie, at Dogtown, near Lookout Point *below and top right.*
Telephone cables line the margin of a snow-sprinkled dirt road *center.*
Bottom pictures: snow lies patchily on the Killdeer Badlands, seen from Seventy Mile Butte, and storm clouds gather over the prairie landscape, *facing page.*

GROS MORNE

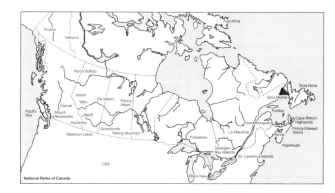

Gros Morne, located on the west coast of Newfoundland's
Great Northern Peninsula, contains some of Canada's most
geologically interesting and spectacular land forms. *Left:*
the cliffs of Green Gardens from Lobster Cove and *above,*
Western Brook Pond.

Below: **the might of Bakers Brook Falls seen from the air.** *Right:* **the boardwalk and** *facing page* **the wind-rippled surface of one of the ponds on the trail to Western Brook Pond. The remaining pictures show three different aspects of the cliffs and coastline at Green Gardens.**

The view *left* towards Lobster Cove Head Lighthouse – just
visible behind the trees at left center – with Green Gardens
in the distance. *Above:* horses enjoying the tidal pools on
the beach in St. Paul's Bay.

JASPER

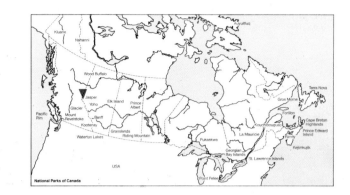

Waters reflect the blue of the sky and the colors of the
clouds at Medicine Lake *above* and Maligne Lake *left*.

The Athabasca Glacier *these pages* lies at the southern end of Jasper National Park, near the Icefield Center. The center offers information, slide shows and guided walks with park naturalists.

Clouds almost obscure Mushroom Peak and the Athabasca Valley *facing page,* **and Tangle Ridge** *top left* **across the Sunwapta River from Icefields Parkway.** *Above right:* **dawn breaks on the Athabasca and Dome glaciers seen from Wilcox Pass.** *Top right:* **the Athabasca River and Valley, near Jasper, and** *above left* **mountain goats at Disaster Point mineral salt lick.**

Huge rocks mimic the shapes of the Opal Hills behind
Medicine Lake, seen at dawn *right*. Angel Glacier, on the
slopes of Mount Edith Cavell, just catches the first rays of
morning sunlight *above*.

Water runs off the rocks *left,* **of Maligne Canyon to join the rushing Maligne River.** *Above:* **Maligne Lake offers many and varied vistas to the explorer.**

KEJIMKUJIK

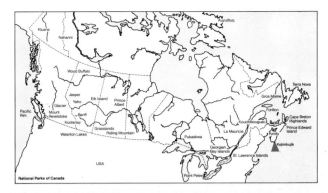

National Parks of Canada

Most of the park's waters are dark brown in color, stained by the bogs they flow through. The rich forestation lining the banks of rivers is deceptive: almost the entire area has been burned or logged within the last 200 years. *Left:* **Mill Falls on the Mersey River** *above.*

Waterways are the essence of Kejimkujik. The lake of the same name is one of the largest in the province, and unequaled for canoeing. These woods and rivers were the seasonal home of the nomadic Micmac Indians for hundreds of years before the first Europeans came to Canada. Where the trees overhang the still waters, a special kind of peace is created. *Left, bottom left and far left:* participants in an interpretation paddle in the evening on the Mersey River. *Top left:* canoeists near Jake's Landing, and *below* children enjoying Kejimkujik Lake, at Kedge Beach.

Hardly a ripple disturbs the waters of Kejimkujik Lake *above* save for the gentle wake of a slow-moving canoe. *Top left:* pickerel weed at the edge of the Mersey River. *Left and far left:* Kejimkujik Lake pictured near Merrymakedge. *Facing page:* trees overhang a quiet stretch of the Mersey River.

White-tail deer *right, bottom right and facing page;* **the uncomfortable-looking porcupine** *far right and bottom left* **and the spruce grouse** *below* **form a small sample of the wildlife that inhabits or visits Kejimkujik.**

A **canoe** *facing page* breaks the reflections in the waters of the Mersey River in the late evening light.

Floating heart plants pattern the water of Kejimkujik Lake *top right* **as does the extensive growth of water lilies** *bottom left.*

Nectar is sipped from a Rosepogonia orchid *bottom right* **while** *top left* **is an example of the rare coastal plain plant, meadow beauty.**

KLUANE

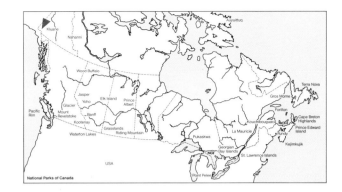

Clouds fill the sky, *left,* **above Kluane's St. Elias Mountain Range.**
Above: **the sun sets beyond the far shore of Kathleen Lake.**

The eroded face of Kluane's Goat Mountain *above* viewed from St. Elias Lake. *Facing page:* the deep blue of the evening sky is seen in the waters of a tributary feeding St. Elias Lake.

Red Castle Ridge *top left and left* **lit by the early morning sun and** *above* **shrouded in cloud, from Sheep Bullion Plateau. Also from the plateau may be seen the peaks of the Vulcan Mountain Ranges** *far left.*
 Glacial Hummock Lake *facing page* **at the toe of the Kaskawulsh Glacier, on the Kaskawulsh Glacier floor.**

The panorama *above* shows the Slims River from Mount
Vulcan Sub Alpine Plateau with the Kluane Range in the
background. Frost-sculptured rocks *facing page* on Mount
Vulcan, with the Kaskawulsh Valley Glacier forcing its
inexorable way as it carves the floor of the valley.

Gribble Gulch *right* is a small stream fed by glacial run-off from the St. Elias Mountains, seen in the background.

Glacial ice *far right* litters the shore of a hummock lake at the terminal of the Kaskawulsh glacier with, in the background, Mount Vulcan.

Below: a sweeping panorama of the Alsek Valley at sunset.

Bottom right: the upper peaks of the Kaskawulsh Mountain Ranges seen from the Mount Vulcan Sub-Alpine Plateau.

Facing page: Mount Maxwell, the highest peak of the Kaskawulsh ranges, lit by the midsummer evening sun.

KOOTENAY

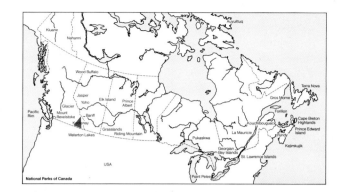

Left: a view of Vermilion Fire Burn showing the dead trees that resulted after a forest fire ravaged the area. All visitors to the national parks are urged to be careful with fires. *Above,* a close-up of the same burn on the slopes of Stanley Peak.

Mount Harkin, *left,* is seen here surrounded by
neighboring peaks, their snowy heads reflected in waters
painted by sky colors. *Above,* a view of the same
mountains taken from a different angle.

Facing page: **a bull moose in the lower stretches of the Vermilion Fire Burn;** *below,* **a watchful coyote.** *Left* **is shown the view from McLeod Meadows looking across the Kootenay River. The potholes** *bottom left* **were carved by the waters of the Vermilion River.** *Bottom,* **a scene at the treeline, near Stanley Glacier.**

KOUCHIBOUGUAC

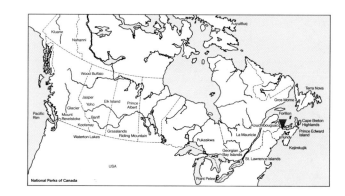

These aerial views of Kouchibouguac show very clearly
the dunes, north of Kelly's Beach, *above* and Kelly's Beach
and the extensive boardwalk *left*.

Left: **Tern Island and the southern end of Kelly's Beach seen from the air. On the Kouchibouguac River, near the boat house, the late afternoon sun** *below* **gives way to a golden sunset** *bottom left and facing page,* **where canoeists take advantage of the last moments of daylight to create a timeless scene. Snaking through the lush vegetation is Kelly's Bog Trail,** *bottom right.*

Common terns fill the sky, *facing page,* above Tern Island. *Top, far right:* the somewhat untidy-looking nest of the common tern, complete with three eggs. *Bottom left:* a tern chick 'plays dead', lying still and quiet in an attempt to avoid its enemies' interest. The osprey *bottom right* nests in the park and has become its symbol. Park wardens *top left* on boat patrol in St. Louis Bay. *Top center:* a stranded jellyfish at the edge of Kelly's Beach.

LA MAURICIE

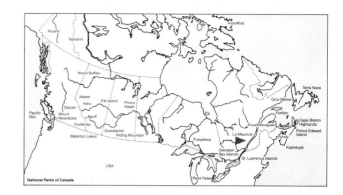

National Parks of Canada

Canoeists *left* paddle the peaceful waters at the southern
end of Lake Wapizagonke and *above*, a riot of autumn
colors blanket the slopes at Lac à Saur.

La Mauricie offers beautiful beaches for swimming and surfing such as at Lake Edouard *below* and Lac à la Pêche *bottom right*, from where the park warden is seen going about his duties.

There is no doubt that canoeing *right and facing page* and canoe camping are among the most popular activities.

All the seasons have their attractions and winter transforms the park into a different world. There is little doubt, however, that most people would find the glorious colors of fall, *these pages*, breathtakingly beautiful.

A lazy sky softens and transforms the landscape seen from Le Passage lookout, *left.* Burnished reds and yellows of early autumn splash fire among the greens of trees at Lac à Sam, *top.* Some aspects of the park such as the location of the waterfall *above* are not publicized because of the fragility of the environment. *Right:* true wilderness – Lac en Croix Brook.

Reflections of grasses and rocks in the mirror-like waters of Alphonse Lake *above*. At this point Caribou Brook *right* lies almost hidden by the thick vegetation on all sides.

MOUNT REVELSTOKE

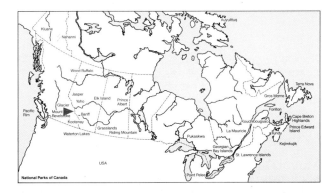

Winding its way through the forest *left* is the boardwalk of Mount Revelstoke's Giant Cedars Trail, where growths of devil's club *above* here display autumnal shades.

Facing page: **While sundown casts a purple glow over the land, the full moon emerges above the mountains, a common sight in a region where the sun is early hidden by the peaks. Ice Box Gorge,** *right,* **and the Revelstoke Mountains in the background.**

Fall colours surround the bright red berries of a mountain ash, *below,* **pictured on the Eva and Miller Lakes Trail.** *Bottom right:* **Eva Lake and Mount Williamson Ridge.**

NAHANNI

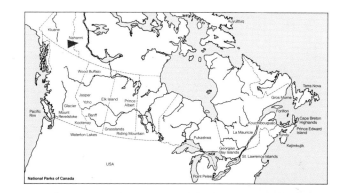

The glancing rays of the setting sun highlight clumps of
cottongrass *left* on the floor of Prairie Creek. The heavy
smoke of a forest fire almost obscures Nahanni Butte
Mountains in the background *above*.

A forest fire *facing page* on the border of Nahanni Park. Not necessarily as destructive as they may appear, fires can play an important part in the ecology of the forest. The Sluice Box Rapids System *bottom left* lies immediately before Virginia Falls, seen *top left* with characteristic mid-morning rainbow and *top right* at "night": this region has long periods of daylight in summer. *Above:* an army campsite downriver from Virginia Falls.

Facing page: **canoes and rafts at rest beneath the towering face of the aptly-named Pulpit Rock.**

Supplies being unloaded *top left* **from a Sea Otter floatplane near Virginia Falls in preparation for a raft trip** *bottom left and right* **to Nahanni Butte Indian Settlement. A rainbow** *above* **across the foot of Virginia Falls.**

On the Nahanni River, rafts encountering white water *right* at Rafferty's Riffle, First Canyon, and *below left* in Second Canyon. A peaceful river and wooded mountain slopes *bottom right* form an idyllic setting at the entrance to Deadmen Valley. *Facing page:* rafts leaving Third Canyon, immediately before Morengo Creek.

Canoers and rafters seen on these pages note the smoke that is shrouding the area around First Canyon as the forest continues to burn.

PACIFIC RIM

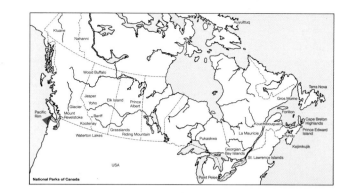

The glory of sunset across the gently rolling sea at Green Point *above* **and at Long Beach** *left* **creates scenes in Pacific Rim National Park that are as timeless as the setting sun itself.**

Purples and violets of the dawn reflected *above* in a tidal
pool at Pacific Rim's Schooner Cove.
Facing page: the twisted and gnarled stump of a dead
cedar at Grice Bay.

Driftwood on the rocks at dawn, South Beach *above* **and at sunset** *facing page.*

A characteristic of all coastal areas in Canada is the tide and the influence it has on shoreline life. Here, *above*, low tide uncovers a variety of small organisms. *Facing page:* gulls are tidal feeders, seen here hunting for small fish.

Sea anemones *above* lying in a shallow tidal pool at Pacific
Rim's Cox Point and *facing page* sculpted headlands at
Chesterman Beach.

The incoming sea temporarily reclaims the rocks and tidal pools of a small pocket beach *above* near Sealion Rocks on the West Coast Trail.

From Clarke Island, looking through the Broken Group Islands *right* towards the Vancouver Island coastline.

Western red cedars and amabalis firs are shown *top right*, seen from the Rain Forest Trail.

Facing page: the southernmost point of Broken Group Islands, with Vancouver Island in the background.

At sundown, the land and the sea change, as shown by the tidal pool photographed during early morning, on page 172, and the same scene taken just before sunset, *above*. *Facing page:* moisture is a dominant influence on the west coast of Canada; mist often shrouds the land and the water, rising slowly on still days and putting down a milky fog on the sea and distant shores; here, at Sealion Rocks.

A fishing boat, *left,* runs through the fog-shrouded waters of the Broken Group Islands. *Below,* a view of Ucluelet harbor. *Right,* bald eagles constantly scan the waters for fish, the main prey of these great birds. *Bottom, left and right,* a female killer whale seen soon after it has risen, blown and taken a new breath. *Center,* a beacon light on Broken Group Islands.

POINT PELEE

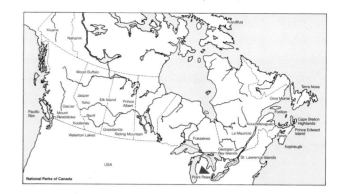

**Point Pelee is Canada's southernmost region. Seen from the
air above Lake Erie is Red Head Pond** *above* **and some of
the many species of trees found in the park** *left.*

Above: sunset over Point Pelee's changeable marshland *facing page.* Under the canopy of the trees *top center* and in the dunes and open meadows, *right and top left,* wild flowers grow profusely; poppies and wild puccoon are among the species to be found. *Top right:* a splintered and weathered tree root on East Beach.

Driftwood, seagulls and fishermen gather at Point Pelee, its tip pointing across the waters to the United States, far over the horizon, *these pages.*

Point Pelee is a living museum of natural history which contains many and varied species of plant and animal life such as the Canada anemones, *bottom left*, the painted turtle *far right* and Blanding's turtle *bottom right and facing page*, some of which can at times be observed from the boardwalk *below*.

PRINCE ALBERT

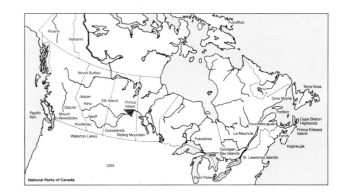

Morning light on the Waskesiu River and *left* **a roadside pond near the Heart Lakes in Saskatchewan's Prince Albert National Park.**

Right: **a beaver lodge on Amiskowan Lake and** *far right* **the view from the Shady Lake lookout.** *Below:* **towards Shady Lake from "Height-of-Land" firetower.** *Bottom right* **is a creek leading from Shady Lake to Amiskowan Lake.** *Facing page:* **the fury of an electrical storm as it passes over Halkett Lake.**

Cattails growing in a creek *above* leading from Shady Lake to Amiskowan Lake. *Facing page:* a beaver lodge constructed at the edge of Amiskowan Lake.

Better photographs than these of a beaver at work would be hard to come by. It should be noted that although the beaver cuts through a lot of wood, it only eats the bark of the trees that it downs. In

middle picture, *left*, the beaver pauses for a snack of newly-cut poplar bark – which tastes rather like cucumber.

168

Late evening across South Bay *above* **and looking towards King Island** *facing page*, **on Waskesiu Lake.**

Above, a fiery sky over the trees lining the shore of
Waskesiu Lake and *right* **Waskesiu River just after dawn.**

Top left, **a red squirrel;** *above:* **the great horned owl;** *top center and facing page:* **plains bison** *(Bison bison); top right:* **barred owl** *and right:* **white-tail deer.**

The Kingsmere River *above right* carries its water to the sandy-shored Kingsmere Lake *above left*. Reflections of trees in a roadside pond *top left* near the Heart Lakes, and Ajawaan Lake *top right* on the shores of which stands Grey Owl's cabin, *facing page*, where he did much of his writing.

The view, *left,* shows the extent of wooded land within the park, photographed from Boundary Fire Tower. *Above:* first-growth aspen leave room within their ranks for profuse shrubs and flowers while at right, the aspen have closed ranks, allowing little light to reach the forest floor. The spruces in the lower background have, however, managed to gain a foothold in the aspen domain.

PRINCE EDWARD ISLAND

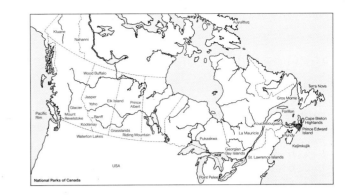

The easily-eroded red sandstone cliffs of Prince Edward Island are readily apparent in the view *left* towards Orby Head. Further along the shore the sandstone gives way to shore *above* at Rustico Beach.

Under the influence of storm waves and winds, barrier islands formed by the breaking down of sandstone rubble migrate shorewards, resulting in the extensive beaches such as Ross Lane Beach *right and below.* The beach sand is then driven further inshore by wind action and trapped by marram grass, resulting in the formation of the coastal dunes.

Facing page: the Stanhope Cape lighthouse stands starkly white against the clear blue sky. The "Dalvay-by-the-Sea" hotel is shown *bottom right* in its setting by Dalvay Lake.

Broken red sandstone rubble litters the shore *far left* near Orby Head and *left* near Cavendish.

Dwarfed by the rocks on which they stand and the incoming waves, two cormorants *below* pictured at Orby Head, where the sun casts its strong glare across the sea *bottom left. Right:* some of the island's many species of grasses and wild flowers, here seen on the clifftop at Cape Turner.

185

Vacationers *facing page* make full use of the fine weather and the facilities of Cavendish Main Beach.

How fine the balance between existence and extinction of so many species of wildlife and how necessary our awareness of it: this is something about which the park services constantly strive to inform people. An example of an endangered species is the piping plover, *this page,* defending its chick and egg on Cavendish Sandspit.

The huge ball of the sun appears to rest delicately on the horizon *left* at sunset from Cavendish Beach *below*. Just along the coast from Cavendish Beach the waves eat inexorably at the soft red sandstone *bottom*.

Green Gables House *facing page* is located at the western end of the park in Cavendish. This lovely farmhouse is known to millions of readers through Lucy Maud Montgomery's classic novel, *Anne of Green Gables*.

PUKASKWA

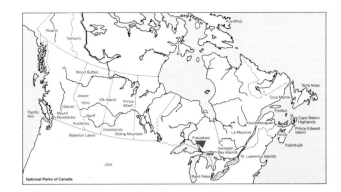

"A Wild Shore on an Inland Sea." The 'wild shore' is the
Canadian Shield and the 'inland sea' is Superior – the
largest of the Great Lakes. It is these factors that give
Pukaskwa – pronounced Púk-a-saw – its wild fascination.

"Superior is a sea: she breeds storms and rain and fog like the sea . . . She is wild, masterful and dreaded." The Reverend George Grant's words are all too apparent when viewing the storm-tossed debris hurled on the shores of Lake Superior *these pages* following a storm.

Pukaskwa National Park, on the shores of Lake Superior, has been described as having 'wild, awesome and fascinating appeal'. In this wilderness live, in addition to the black bear *left*, moose, wolf, woodland caribou and many other, smaller animals.

Far left and below right is a quiet creek at the head of Hattie Cove, on the Coastal Hiking Trail; *bottom left* is the cove's shoreline while *facing page* is the oddly-named Onion Island, also in Hattie Cove.

Above: a scene in the Boreal Forest – which contains spruce, fir, birch, poplar, jack pine, tamarack and aspen – on Southern Headland. *Facing page:* the evening sky streaked with gold and violet across Horseshoe Beach towards Superior's Pic Island and Ogilvy Point.

RIDING MOUNTAIN

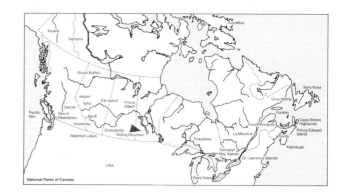

These pages: **the road to Lake Audy makes its way through pure stands of trembling aspen and balsam poplars, the leaves of the trees gold in the early morning sun.**

The reds, yellows and golds of fall at Ominnik Marsh *above*
contrast with the ominous build-up of heavy storm clouds
over Clear Lake, *facing page.*

Autumn leaves *left and above* **gather at the water's edge along Dead Ox Creek on the 'Burls and Bittersweet' trail. A snowshoe hare,** *above right*, **attempts to blend with the surrounding vegetation.**

Frosted undergrowth *bottom* by a beaver pond in the west of Riding Mountain Park. The plains buffalo *below* should feel at home here as skeletal remains indicate that herds once roamed the area. *Right:* 'The Bench' above Birdtail Valley with discarded elk antlers in the foreground. *Facing page:* on the highland plateau, near Highway 10.

Magnificently gnarled and convoluted roots of a pine, *left,* **force their way through and around the rocks at the water's edge on Endymion Island.** *Above:* **the shaded floor of a forest on Hill Island.**

Above and top left: **the Thousand Islands/Ivy Lea Bridge crossing over Georgina and Constance Islands, from Hill Island.** *Top, facing page and above left:* **aerial shots of some of the richly-forested islands in the St. Lawrence River that make up this remarkable national park.**

Great blue herons nesting in the St. Lawrence Islands National Park. The great blue is the largest of the heron family and wades in shallow water, catching fish and water animals with a swift jab of its bill.

Rocks thrust from the ground on Mermaid Island like jumbled gravestones in a country churchyard and beech maples almost meet overhead in a forest on Hill Island, *facing page. Far left:* hairy beardtongue on West Grenadier Island and a wood lily puts out its flower. Dearberries on West Grenadier Island, *below.*

Boats moored *below* at the landing stage on Georgina Island with the Ivy Lea Bridge soaring overhead in the background and at night mooring on Camelot Island, *bottom right.*

Bottom left: a night view of the 'National Parks Showboat' at Mermaid Island and *left* part of the island's rocky coastline. *Bottom center* is Halfmoon Bay, on Bostwick Island and *right*, wind-blown white pines are silhouetted against the cloud-filled sky.

TERRA NOVA

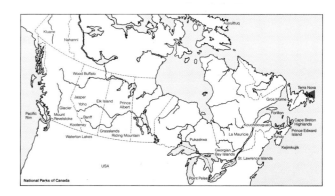

A crescent moon hangs over the trees of a forest *left* near
Big Brook, and the setting sun catches highlights on the
waves in Newman Sound *above*.

Carnivorous plants do not devour their prey by chewing but, after trapping insects, they subject them to the decomposing actions of digestive enzymes, bacteria or both. Most carnivorous species are green plants that manufacture food in the normal way by photosynthesis from the raw materials of sunlight, water and carbon dioxide in the presence of chlorophyll, and they are not, therefore, sustained by the animal diet alone. *Above:* the pitcher plant, the flower emblem of Newfoundland, and *facing page,* the sundew plant.
Above right: Ochre Hill Pond and *right,* cladonia lichen ('British soldiers').

Far left: **rock formations, and** *left,* **fishermen bringing home their catch, in Newman Sound.**

Moonrise *bottom left* **over the Terra Nova landscape.**

Rocks on the shores of Salton's Brook Cove highlighted by the evening sun *below* **and,** *facing page,* **a beaver pond at Burnt Point.**

WATERTON LAKES

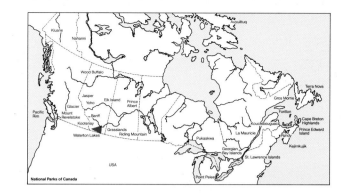

In a timeless scene *left* buffalo graze the prairie in Waterton Lakes
National Park. A view *above* of the prairie land rolling towards the
Waterton Lakes Mountains.

The snow-dusted Livingstone Mountains rise sheer behind Cameron Lake *top left* while snow covers the shoreline of Summit Lake *left*. The scene *above* shows the weathered roots of a dead spruce with Vimy Ridge in the background behind Upper Waterton Lake.

The stunning view *right* is of Blakiston Valley from the Mount Crandell viewpoint, looking towards Waterton Lake.

Above: the southern reaches of the Rocky Mountains reflected in a waterhole at Twin Buttes and *facing page* Vimy Ridge (left) and Mount Richards (right) far across Maskinonge Lake.

A fallen tree *above* on the snow-covered shoreline of Summit Lake.
From Bear's Hump Ridge may be seen the buildings of Waterton Park
townsite on the shores of Upper Waterton Lake, *facing page.*

At the entrance to Waterton Lakes is Buffalo Paddock where, against a mountainous backdrop, buffalo graze the prairie.

The waters of a stream in Red Rock Canyon, in the Blakiston Valley, flow over a multi-colored bed *left and facing page.*
  A doe mule deer grazes at Cameron Lake *top* and, *above* a lone bull bison pictured in the rutting season.

WOOD BUFFALO

The vegetation of the Salt Plains *left* is composed of a variety of salt-resistant species. *Above:* Karst Sinkhole, near Carlson's Firetower. Sinkholes are created by surface and ground water dissolving the bedrock.

A meadow of giant dandelions *above* on a low-lying island in Lake Claire Narrows, Peace Point, on the Athabasca Delta. *Right:* sunset from the banks of Peace River, Peace Point Indian Reserve.

Right: **the backwash of a fishing boat foams the waters of the Peace River.**
Below and facing page: **willow grass reed beds at the mouth of the Mamalaw Lake.**
Below right: **a lone buffalo bull chewing the cud.**

Wood Buffalo Park contains the largest free-roaming herd
of bison in the world. On these pages are seen only a few
of the bison that shelter within this huge park.

Autumnal dawns in the northern wilderness are spectacles
that reward the early riser. *Above*, the sun is just emerging
above the treeline, reflecting itself in the Slave River;
facing page, arrival of daylight is forecast by sluggish mist
rising from the water while the sun remains hidden.

Evening sunlight on a stand of trembling aspen *facing page*
on the banks of the Peace River, Peace Point Indian
Reserve. *Above:* dehydrated salt mounds on the salt plains
of Wood Buffalo Park resemble frozen patches of snow.

YOHO

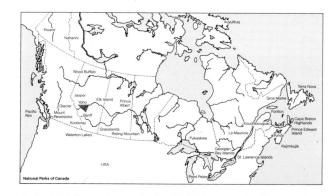

Alpine silt deposits in western lakes create the beautiful aquamarine tints demonstrated *left* **by the waters of Schaeffer Lake; in the background is Schaeffer Mountain.** *Above:* **fast, turbulent waters are commonplace in Yoho National Park. This picture was taken at Natural Bridge.**

The rail lines pass through spiral tunnels, *top left; bottom left and top right* are two views of Mount Lefroy; *bottom, right* shows the barren slopes of Mount Yukness. *Facing page:* Schaeffer Lake, surrounded by forbidding peaks.

The snows of autumn blanket the Mount Odaray Plateau Grand View
above and facing page.

Left: the Leauchoil Hoodoos (glacial formations) with Chancellor Peak in the background.

The view *below left* is of Lefroy Lake, one of three tier lakes linking lakes O'Hara and Oesa. *Below:* O'Hara Falls with (at lower right) the emerald waters of Lake O'Hara.

Facing page: Lake Oesa, ringed by mounts Lefroy and Yukness.

Wapta Falls, *left,* pictured at dusk from the logging road. The still waters of Emerald Lake *above* with, behind it, Emerald Peak (left) and Mount Carnarvon (right).

Above right: the lace-like beauty of Takakkaw Falls.